Young Abraham Lincoln:

The Childhood and Early Life of Abraham Lincoln

By Howard Brinkley

BookCaps™ Study Guides

www.bookcaps.com

Table of Contents

About HistoryCaps

HistoryCaps is an imprint of BookCaps™ Study Guides. With each book, a brief period of history is recapped. We publish a wide array of topics (from baseball and music to science and philosophy), so check our growing catalogue regularly (www.bookcaps.com) to see our newest books.

Introduction

The Lincoln family can be traced to a group of brothers—Samuel, Daniel, and Thomas—who came to Massachusetts from England between 1635 and 1645. Interestingly enough, the family tree has an impressive number of "public service" branches. Samuel Lincoln's great-great grandson Levi was a Minuteman, a legislator, and represented Massachusetts in the Senate. He later became United States Attorney General to President Thomas Jefferson and Secretary of State to President James Madison. Levi's son, of the same name, became the Governor of Maine and another son, Enoch, served in Congress and became the Governor of Maine. The Lincolns were likely descendants of Quakers, described as "a serene, peaceable, obstinate people."[i]

As a child, the young Abraham may have heard stories of his paternal grandfather and namesake, Abraham Lincoln, who also descended from Samuel Lincoln. He would have heard the story of how he was an early pioneer and farmer, and one of the more wealthy ones of the time. He may have learned of the senior Abraham's friendship with the family of one Daniel Boone, who convinced him to sell his farm in Virginia in 1780 and move to Kentucky. During this time, clearing a farm in the Kentucky territory was dangerous business. Indians were a constant threat, and in fact most families were required to live in or near army forts or stations for protection. Most assuredly Lincoln would have been told the alarming story of how in 1788, while working the fields on his farm, his grandfather was shot and killed by an Indian, while his sons watched helplessly. As Lincoln's father Thomas, only ten years old at the time, watched the life leave his father's body, his eldest brother Mordecai quickly ran to the cabin, retrieved a rifle, and put a bullet in the lone Indian who had now descended upon his younger brothers. The boys were saved but no doubt forever scarred by the life-changing event.

In fact, while the eldest son Mordecai inherited most of the estate, young Thomas, with no portion, would become something of a drifter. He hired himself out as a farmhand, and often worked alongside slaves receiving the same wage, about three shillings a day. He became skilled at farm work and somewhere along the way learned carpentry, but was not extremely ambitious. Though illiterate, he was described as a quiet, moral, and religious man. Perhaps ready to "settle down" at age 25, he purchased a farm in Hardin County, Kentucky. He married Nancy Hanks on June 12, 1806.

If Tom's family was marked by tragedy, Nancy's was a picture of dysfunction. She was an illegitimate child whose mother shuffled her around to live with one relative or another most of her life. Her maternal grandparents raised her for a while until her grandfather died. She returned to live with her mother, who had married by this time, but only until another relative could be found to take her in. Despite the hardships she endured—seemingly serious enough to damage to a child's psyche—she managed to be, by nearly all accounts, a good wife and mother. The Lincolns welcomed their first child Sarah (called Sally) into the world on February 10, 1807.

Chapter 1: Life in Kentucky

Tom Lincoln's first farm in Sinking Spring, Kentucky was once described as "a small valley farm, with not more than twelve to fifteen acres of any kind of tillable land"[ii] and said to be covered with scrubby underbrush. Nancy Lincoln was reportedly ashamed of the way they lived in those days, especially that Tom never took the time to put a floor in their cabin. But, she thought that he was doing his best to keep them fed and didn't dwell on it.

Besides the struggles just to produce crops on the barren land, there were struggles with land titles and ownership disputes aplenty. The surveying techniques used then were "troubled." These were English methods, with metes and bounds, and seemed to work well for seldom traded parcels, but in the Kentucky frontier, transactions were many and frequent and property lines became confused. Tom had very little patience for this, and after three years of coaxing crops from the Sinking Spring property, decided to expand his horizons in search of greener pastures.

In 1808, Thomas Lincoln purchased his second farm in Kentucky on the south fork of Nolin Creek, about eighteen miles southeast of Elizabethtown, for $200 cash. This brought his land holdings to 586½ acres in total, including two land lots in Elizabethtown. It was here at Nolin Creek that Nancy Lincoln gave birth to their first son, Abraham. The family's home at the time was a tiny one room log cabin with a dirt floor, one door, no windows, and not much protection from the elements, with large cracks allowing in rain, snow, wind, and mosquitoes. The family likely slept on a mattress of dried leaves. After two years on the Nolin Creek farm, they moved to a farm on Knob Creek, about ten miles away.

The new farm included bottomland and was much more fertile than the Nolin Creek property. This farm is the one that Abraham would later say was his first recollection, describing it as "knobby as a piece of land could be, with deep hollows, ravines—cedar trees…as thick as trees could grow."[iii]

The year 1812 brought misfortune and war. A second son, Thomas, was born and lived only a few days. Tom Lincoln had fought in earlier wars against Indians, but when the War of 1812 dawned, he was a family man and did not enlist. Nevertheless, he always had a great amount of respect for soldiers and went out of his way to offer food or meet other needs upon crossing paths with them. His son Abraham would always remember the kind way he treated the soldiers whenever they came around, and indeed had his own story to tell. When he was just a lad and had been fishing, he was walking home with his catch of the day, a single fish. He happened to meet a soldier and, remembering his father's treatment of the soldiers, gave him the fish.

As the children grew, there was no shortage of chores and hard work. At some point in Lincoln's childhood, a cousin of Nancy Lincoln, Dennis Hanks, came to live with them in the tiny cabin. Dennis was about ten years older than Abraham and surely would have been a good hand on the farm, while also providing companionship to the young Abraham. Life in pioneer days brought chores galore, and the children would not have been exempt. As a small boy, some of the chores Abraham may have been responsible for were fetching water, filling the wood box, cleaning ashes from the fireplace, running errands, and hoeing rows and rows of the main corn crop, with smaller plantings of beans, onions, and potatoes to work. Before he was able to handle a plow, Abraham would likely have done some "corn dropping" whereby small hills of earth were formed and a few seeds dropped in. By the age of seven, he would be learning to plow.

While young Abraham had his share of chores and would have worked alongside his father to learn farm work, his life was not devoid of distractions and a little fun. With an older cousin in the house and a neighbor friend named Austin Gollaher, he got into all manner of mischief. The story is told of a Sunday afternoon when Mrs. Gollaher had called on the Lincolns and the two boys were running the woods when they found themselves beside a swollen creek. Neither could swim but they took a notion to cross the creek on a narrow foot log in search of some partridges. Inevitably, Abraham fell in and quick-thinking Austin grabbed a long pole and held it out to him. He was able to grab it and be pulled in, though he had taken in more than a little water and was nearly unconscious when he got to the bank. His friend "rolled and pounded him in good earnest,"[iv] and he soon came to. It was quite a scare for both boys and they vowed not to let their mothers find out for fear of a whipping, something which apparently both boys had personally experienced. But their wet clothes would surely give them away! Not to worry, the two stripped their clothing and spread it on the rocks in the warm summer sun. Indeed, the boys avoided their whipping, and the story was not told until many years later after Lincoln's death.

Chapter 2: Education

Schooling in those days could be called "hit or miss." Abraham and Sally would have walked approximately four miles to the log schoolhouse with a dirt floor, but only when a schoolmaster could be found and the children could be spared from the farm. Teachers were usually men, and very often religious men who would teach only until a better job could be found, so there were no regular school terms. The main requirement of teachers, in fact, was to be strong enough to "handle" the older boys, who seemed prone to fighting and other mischief. Parents would be responsible both for boarding and paying the schoolmaster, usually with wild game or produce from their farms. For this reason, education was obtained by methods other than just traditional schooling, and was very much dependent upon parents, other influences, and perhaps the degree to which a child wanted to learn. For education, while somewhat elusive in those days, could be gotten, and Abraham Lincoln figured just how to do it.

Two early schoolmasters who taught Lincoln were Zachariah Riney and Caleb Hazel. Little is known of either man, except that they were both denizens of the area, not drifters, and are credited with teaching Lincoln to read and write. Most likely when he did attend school, it would be one known as a "blab school" in which students would read their lessons aloud in class to show that they were actually studying. The children would read simultaneously, and if one got louder and faster, they all eventually did. But it was considered a tried and true method of learning in those days. His friend Austin Gollaher spoke of Abraham as a very bright and fast learner, saying that he would study hard, even chopping up Spicewood brushes to burn for light so that he could study at night.

ı Thomas Lincoln was illiterate, he
ı to want better for his son. Nancy Lincoln valued reading and education, and read to her children from the Bible, probably one of the few books in the Lincoln, or any other, household at the time. She also told them the fairy tales and legends that she knew. Dennis Hanks recalled that she had a Webster's spelling book that she used to teach Abraham and Sally the alphabet and to read a little. Another book that was a standard in the Kentucky territory was Murray's English Reader, which explained how to read different types of writing, and Abraham would describe this as a most useful book. Although there are conflicting opinions as to how much Tom Lincoln encouraged Abraham in his reading and education, his mother and later his stepmother were always said to be greatly supportive of his ambitions in this regard, and he neglected no opportunity to learn. His parents taught him the early American ideal that an upright and industrious boy can aspire to most anything. It would eventually become apparent that the early teachers who took the time to teach him, the fertile mind of the young Abraham, and his raw attraction to books and stories would become the perfect storm for a pioneer education.

Though the formal education Abraham received was referred to as desultory, he nevertheless learned not only to read, but to comprehend and think on what he read. He is known to have read several specific books through the years, including the Bible, which most families owned. Others included *Pilgrim's Progress*, *Aesop's Fables*, *Robinson Crusoe*, and Weems's *Life of Washington*, and he knew them all very well. After reading *Life of Washington*, he became enamored of George Washington and read the book over and over; in fact, he would later make reference to the book in political speeches. He was constantly in search of new books, and once made the statement that he "read through every book he had ever heard of in that country, for a circuit of fifty miles."[v] Many stories are told of Lincoln walking for several miles just to borrow a book he hadn't read, saying "the things I want to know are in books; my best friend is the man who'll git me a book I ain't read."[vi]

One of Lincoln's later schoolmasters, around 1820 when Abraham would have been eleven years old, was Andrew Crawford, who was a justice of the peace and determined to teach his students some manners. Upon entering the schoolhouse door, boys were to remove their hats and bow; girls were to curtsy. Even during play time, children were expected to stop their games and give the same salutation to passersby. Students were also taught to make proper introductions. In 1822, Lincoln's second Indiana school teacher was James Swaney, about which little is known. About four years later, Azel Dorsey taught him for a time, in the first and only public school Lincoln attended, with all expenses paid by the government instead of parents. Dorsey would say of him, "Abraham Lincoln was one of the noblest boys I ever knew and is certain to become noted if he lives." The teacher was most impressed that Lincoln owned an arithmetic book and would bring it to school, saying that it was rare in those days for students to own these books and was an indication that his family strongly supported his education.

Dennis Hanks would say of Lincoln that after the age of twelve, he never saw Abraham without a book nearby. If he was heading out for a day of plowing, he would fill his pockets with corn dodgers and put a book inside his shirt. At night he'd pull up a chair by the fireplace and read, and it was said that people could come and go around him, and he would never know of the activity, so engrossed was he in his book. Dennis further remarked that books told Abraham more than they seemed to tell other people. The same could be said of newspapers, which Abraham became just as passionate about and thirsty for as he grew older. Anyone could read a news article, but Abraham would ponder it and talk about it while working in the fields, posing questions to the other workers or, in their absence, to the corn and beans. Questions like, Who deserves to complain the most, the Indian or the Negro? Sure, his relatives knew and expected this, but what must other workers have thought of this young, deep thinker? How did they respond, or did they?

He would take notes when he read, sometimes using a turkey buzzard quill and brier-root ink when no other option was available. If he had no paper, he would write on boards or logs, both quotations from his books and ciphers. When he was able to write his ciphers, or sums, on paper he would keep them, as though he may want to read through them again. Abraham always kept a book by his bed, reading just before falling to sleep at night and again at first light.

As much as Abraham Lincoln was fascinated by reading and books, he was just as fascinated with writing. Besides writing on paper and any old board he could find, he would also take the opportunity to write in sand, dust, and snow. He would use charcoal to write on the fire shovel, then rub it off and start again. He seemed captivated by the sight of his own name in written form, and the following conversation is recorded between Lincoln and his companion Denny Hanks after he had written his name, "Denny, look at that will you? Abraham Lincoln! That stands for me. Don't look a blamed bit like me!" And according to Denny, Abe would "stand and study it a spell."[vii] Lincoln was also known for writing in verse like this:

Good boys who to their books apply

Will all be great men by and by.

And this…

Abraham Lincoln is my nam [sic]

And with my pen I wrote the same

I wrote in both hast and speed

And left it here for fools to read

Abraham Lincoln his hand and pen

He will be good but god knows when.

From a very early age, all who knew him recognized in him a determination to excel and a gift for writing both prose and poetry. Lincoln found other ways to practice his reading and writing and to "pick up" education. He became the designated letter writer for family members and neighbors, helping them phrase their letters by asking questions about the purpose of the letter, and rewording sentences for them when they didn't come out just right. Another facet of education in those days was churchgoing and traveling preachers. While many preachers may have been illiterate, they traveled the country and preached the gospel passionately and were well received by the settlers. Abraham would no doubt listen to these preachers spellbound, and is said to have repeated whole sermons after they were gone. He was learning all the time and these sermons would have been his introduction to public speaking.

It seems the young Lincoln became interested in storytelling early on, perhaps from the knee of his mother Nancy when she would read and tell him stories as a small child, though his father Tom was said to be a storyteller in his own right. If Nancy Lincoln was determined that her son would learn to read and write, his stepmother seemed likewise to take up that cause and be a great support to him, encouraging his reading and studying, even shooing away the younger children who would pester him as he sat with his books. Dennis Hanks tells of Sarah Lincoln, "She always said Abe was goin' to be a great man some day. An' she wasn't goin' to have him hindered."[viii]

Chapter 3: Religion

In some ways, the line between education and religion was blurred to non-existent in the early territories. If children were taught by listening to Bible stories and learning to read the Bible, then the teachings of the Bible must have taken root at times. It is well known that most settlers were Christian, having descended from families who came to the country to avoid religious persecution. In fact, Lincoln probably attended church more than school. In the district of Kentucky where the Lincolns settled there were many Roman Catholics, but Tom Lincoln was most certainly not of this persuasion, being described by some as a staunch Baptist. Lincoln helped his father Thomas build the Little Pigeon Baptist Church, near the Lincoln home, and Thomas held several positions in the church. Much of the Lincoln family attended the South Fork Church in the Knob Creek area, but this church was split over the slavery issue. The antislavery preacher William Downs was declared in disorder and forbidden to preach, even in members' homes. At the time, the church allowed membership only to adults and mostly just married adults, as there is evidence that Lincoln's sister Sally was not admitted membership until shortly before her marriage. This may explain why Abraham Lincoln's name did not appear on the church roll, as the family moved away before he reached the age of majority.

Obviously, the church did not provide a nursery for little ones, as Lincoln's stepsister Matilda recalls that when their parents went to church, they stayed at home. While waiting for their parents' return, Abraham would get the family Bible out and read to the children. He would then call out a hymn and they would sing a song or two. After that Abraham would "preach" and the children would listen.

Had the children been in attendance, they would have heard preachers teaching their congregants from the Bible to work hard, save, and be decent people. It seems, in those days, to be "decent" people mostly involved not doing a multitude of things, among them drinking, gambling, loafing, gossiping, and backbiting. The underlying theme of "all things should be done decently and in order" prevailed. Hell would have been described as the place where sinners who did not profess faith in Christ would go and burn eternally. After the church meeting, members would tarry and visit among themselves, discussing the weather, their crops, the settlement, letters received, politics, land titles, Indians and such.

In the 1820's when the Lincolns joined the Little Pigeon Baptist Church, there was rivalry among the various denominations which at times was bitter. This could explain why Abraham never joined a church and didn't attend regularly throughout his life, but it is believed by most that he did later become a deeply religious man and knew the Bible well. He would say himself in later life that he turned to the scriptures for comfort and guidance in difficult times.

Tom later joined the Little Mount Church of antislavery separatist Baptists. According to some accounts, he could read a little of the Bible, and he always said grace at meals. He saw that the family observed the Sabbath; if they couldn't attend Sunday services, they would read the Bible together and perhaps sing a few songs. Besides regular church services, camp meetings were held occasionally and lasted for days. That the Lincoln family attended an antislavery church was no small matter. This part of Kentucky was home to some of the more vigorous debates on the issue of slavery and at this time, churches seemed to be leading the charge.

All of his life, Abraham Lincoln would have been an observer, whether deliberately or not, of Christian people and their ways, chiefly his own father. He would have seen the way they treated other people, how they conducted their business dealings and their own affairs. Whether or not Lincoln ever fully adopted the tenets of the Christian faith, he at least adopted their kind and gentle ways. He once went to the trouble to carry a drunken man on his shoulders to save him from freezing. He was well known for his kind treatment of animals. He was honest to a fault, never cheating anyone either in the work or the money he owed them, and making every effort to live peaceably with all that he came to know.

It could be said that a form of religion in those days was the plethora of superstitions that everyone seemed to live by. It is unknown how this practice was reconciled with the prevailing Christian sentiment, but they seemed to coexist nonetheless. Most believed in witches and wizards. Wizards were believed to have the ability to cure sick livestock and pick up a "charmed" stick that could be used to locate water or other treasures underground. "Faith" doctors could heal people using mysterious ceremonies and sayings. Some seemingly harmless events had hidden meanings and were considered harbingers of bad luck to come. For example, a bird lighting in a window meant that a family member would soon die. A horse's breath on a child would surely result in a case of whooping cough. If a dog crossed a hunter's path, there would be bad luck unless he immediately hooked his two little fingers and pulled tightly until the dog was out of sight. Any important project which was begun on a Friday was doomed to fail.

Perhaps most influential for the early settlers were the phases of the moon, which dictated how and when certain jobs were to be performed. In the "light of the moon," meaning the period when the moon is increasing and rising earlier in the day, certain things were to be planted, namely any above-ground crops, plants and trees. Also during this phase, fences were to be set or else they would sink. Soap could only be made in the light of the moon as well, with the added precautions of being stirred by only one person and in only one direction. Potatoes and other root vegetables were to be planted in the dark of the moon, or the phase when the moon was waning and rising later in the day. Surely Abraham learned to live by these popular rules just as his parents did, which may have contributed to his interest in astronomy.

It is well known that Lincoln took a lifelong stance on temperance, but what is not known is exactly why. Drinking whiskey was common then and most households kept it in supply. He reportedly never liked the taste of liquor, though he would drink at times, perhaps to avoid offending his host or companions, perhaps to meet their approval. Ward Hill Lamon, a personal friend and later bodyguard of Lincoln, remarked that Lincoln was a people-pleaser, saying "The 'people' drank, and Abe was always for doing whatever the 'people' did. All his life he held that whatsoever was popular — the habit or sentiment of the masses — could not be essentially wrong."[ix]

As an older youth and young man, it was said of Lincoln that when he went to church at all, it was to mock or mimic what he saw and heard, and "indeed, it is more than probable that the sort of 'religion' which prevailed among the associates of his boyhood impressed him with a very poor opinion of the value of the article."[x] In Lincoln's New Salem days, he was known to associate with the freethinkers, who would deride the gospel and Jesus. During this time he also read Volney's *The Ruins* as well as Paine's *The Age of Reason*. It was probably during this time that Lincoln wrote what has come to be known as his "little book of infidelity," which somewhat mirrored the thoughts of Volney and Paine and was not at all favorable to Christianity. Close friends of Lincoln's advised him to destroy the writing, thinking that it would put an end to any future political career; in fact it is told that one snatched it from his hands and threw it into the fire.

These views from the early life of Lincoln, along with the fact that he was never an official member of any church, have been used by many to claim that Abraham Lincoln was not a Christian, and there is a wide range of opinions on this. However, as with all generations, the religion of the parents must be studied, tested, and challenged by the children. Lincoln's relationship with his father has been said by many to have been troubled and not altogether pleasant, though Thomas was known to be a Christian and a very religious one. If that is the case, then it would only stand to reason that Abraham would challenge the faith of his father as a rite of passage. Even though he may not have embraced the Christian faith as a child, and in fact disparaged it as a young adult, there is evidence that the man may have had a change of heart in later life.

Some have suggested that Lincoln's politics were his religion. Lamon said of his friend, "He believed in a God, but it was the God of nature—the God of Socrates and Plato, as well as the God of Jacob. He believed in a Bible, but it was the open scroll of the universe; and in a religion clear and well defined, but it was a religion that scorned what he deemed the narrow slavery of verbal inspiration….But he held himself no party to the compromise of the Constitution, nor to any law which recognized the justice of human bondage; and he was therefore free to act as his God and nature prompted."[xi] So it seems that the question of his faith and eternal destiny is left to be settled between Lincoln and his maker.

Chapter 4: Move to Indiana

In 1816, Tom Lincoln picked up and moved his family north, over the Ohio River, to Spencer County, Indiana. Whether it was to escape the slavery issue, or because of his difficulty in dealing with Kentucky's land titles, or simply a hankering of the pioneer spirit, may never be known. Slavery was rearing its ugly head in Kentucky, with over 1,200 slaves on the tax records in Hardin County, one taxpayer owning nearly sixty slaves. Tom Lincoln was against slavery, and was not afraid to say so. In any case, Tom's brother Josiah had already settled his family in Indiana, and letters from him and Austin Lincoln, another relative, gave glowing reports of the new land.

To Abraham, just a boy of seven at the time, it must have seemed a high adventure, if for no other reason than there was a break from the grueling daily chores of running a farm. They traveled by horseback and wagon from Knob Creek to a farm near Little Pigeon Creek and the town of Gentryville, Indiana. Much of the journey was through dense woods, with Tom going ahead of the caravan with an ax and clearing the way, no doubt with the help of little Abraham at times. Upon arriving at the new home, which was not much more than a clearing, Tom and Abraham used their axes to build a pole shed, or half-faced camp as it was called then. This was a three-sided hut with the fourth side open to the wind and elements, where the fire would have burned day and night. The Lincolns may have lived in such a structure for up to a year in the new territory.

When the new home was built, the family moved into another one room (18 by 20 feet) log cabin with a loft and no door, window, or floor. Contrary to popular opinion, residing in a cabin of logs was not a sign of poverty, but simply of expediency and common practice. Many families lived in these types of dwellings, and happily so. Early settlers were surrounded by uncut timber, making these logs the most available and practical building materials. During the building of this particular cabin, one day when Tom was absent from the home, Abraham spotted a flock of wild turkeys approaching. From inside the cabin, he grabbed a gun and shot through a crack and killed one. It is said that he never shot at anything larger, and that "he didn't like shooting to kill and didn't care for a reputation as a hunter."[xii]

Arriving in Indiana, the Lincolns were considered squatters. By the end of 1816, there were enough settlers that Indiana was admitted to the Union, and in 1817 Tom Lincoln officially purchased the property from the government at $2 per acre. Food then was mostly wild game, the vegetables they grew, nuts, wild fruit, and honey when a hive could be found. The cabin would have been lit at night by fire logs, pine knots, or hog fat. The nearest water source, a spring, was almost a mile away. Clothing in those early days in Indiana would have likely been pants of deerskin and caps of coonskin, with shirts and dresses made of whatever fabric was available or could be spun. To construct clothing or bedding from cotton or wool was only possible for those who grew their own cotton and could raise their own sheep without the wolves getting them. During summer months, many of the boys would wear one garment, a long tow-linen shirt, with buckskin moccasins or simply bare feet. Life was quite difficult, and most things were hard to come by.

Nothing was so difficult in the early lives of Abraham and his sister Sally however, than the death of their beloved mother Nancy in 1818, just shortly after arriving in Indiana. She was struck, as many were, with the milk sickness, a terrible, feared disease caused by drinking milk from a cow that had eaten poisonous plants, such as snakeroot. She had nursed several of the sick prior to coming down with the disease herself. The disease was known to take down whole families and villages. For several months the small family grieved together while twelve year old Sally kept house the best she could, and Tom and Abraham settled into farm life once again. Also during the year, Abraham was involved in an accident in which he was kicked by a horse and knocked out. It is told that when the horse hit him, he was saying to her, "Git, you old hussy," with his last word being "Git," and the next morning when he came to, "you old hussy." Though he caused his family quite a scare, he seemed to recover quickly.

After several months, Tom left for Kentucky, promising to return—and return he did, with his new wife Sarah Bush Johnston, a widow with three children of her own. Tom had known Sarah from his childhood in Kentucky, and possible had courted her for a time. Nearly overnight the family grew from three to seven. What an adventure it must have been to learn of your new stepmother and become acquainted with three new siblings, all within the confines of one 18 by 20 foot room!

In 1823, John Hanks, another cousin of Nancy Hanks, came to live with the Lincolns, making a total of nine in the cabin. Nevertheless, Sarah Bush Lincoln bravely took on the responsibility of the household and the raising of two other children besides her own, and the Lincoln children grew to love her as their own mother. What a relief it must have been for young Sally to have the burden of an entire pioneer household removed from her tiny shoulders. It is also told that Sarah may have been a bit more well-to-do than Tom and Nancy Lincoln, having brought with her to the Indiana territory some pieces of sophisticated furniture (including a "fine bureau"), some cooking utensils, forks, and feather bedding. She is even credited with coercing her new husband to make improvements to the cabin, adding a floor and building beds and proper chairs (pronounced "cheers"; to say chairs instead of cheers would be construed as "uppity").

Abraham was said to be large and strong for his years and knew how to handle an ax. At the age of 18, he could hold an ax at the handle's end away from his shoulder in a straight, steady, horizontal line. As he worked alongside his father in Indiana, he would have also learned to use a shovel-plow and a sickle, to drive a team of horses, and to thresh wheat. Thomas also taught him to make cabinets and do woodworking, though Abraham was not fond of the work. On occasion, when Tom could spare him, he would hire Abraham out to neighbors for twenty-five cents a day, which he was required to pay over to his father, according to the law and custom of that day. He reportedly never lacked for work, considering his talent for it, his strength, and his willingness to help even with "women's" chores, like carrying water, making fires, and tending babies!

Many of Abraham's family and neighbors seemed to agree that the boy was not really lazy, but allowed his reading and writing to distract him from work, which most considered unnatural in those days. According to Abraham himself, his father taught him to work, but didn't teach him to love it. Another acquaintance is reported as saying that when he worked, "it was with an ease and effectiveness which compensated his employer for the time he spent in practical jokes and extemporaneous speeches."[xiii]

One of Lincoln's favorite activities of the period was going to mill, perhaps because of the break in the drudgery of everyday life, but almost certainly because of his affinity for seeing new places and sights and enjoying some leisure time. The mills of the day were more or less "self-service." Farmers would load their grain and make their way to the mill—maybe in the next town, maybe farther. The trip itself would have been a distraction and break from the routine. Arriving at the mill meant waiting your turn to use the equipment to grind your own grain, sometimes quite a long wait. During this time, the men and boys would have a chance to get acquainted and interact with each other, often through simple conversations, and sometimes through the art of storytelling. Now, this activity was one that Abraham Lincoln could not only enjoy, but excel at. He could tell stories in his droll manner, and punctuate them with his animated faces. Maybe this was laying the very groundwork for the later public speaking that would be so much a part of his life and legacy.

As Abraham grew, he also developed a liking for the atmosphere and fellowship of the general store in Gentryville. Men would gather there to discuss politics, news, and current events in and around the settlement. While he used this venue at times for his storytelling, and developed a following at that, this is also where he began debating and picking up more than a passing interest in the politics of the day. Even among the older men, he became a respected and able debater. At this time, he would go out of his way to attend a debate, a speech, or a court case for the sheer enjoyment of it.

Abraham borrowed books from William Jones and James Gentry, and he was known to memorize some of Henry Clay's speeches. While doing his farm work, he would sometimes stop working to give his own speeches, causing others and even his father sometimes, to stop working and listen. He may have chosen this particular timing simply because of his captive audience, but others have suggested that he may have enjoyed the power he had over others and wanted to see if his speech was compelling enough that they would stop and listen. For this he would sometimes be punished, because public speaking, no matter the quality, does not get the hoeing done!

William Wood, a neighbor in Indiana, reported that, as a teenager Abraham wrote a political piece and gave it to him, in which he said that "the American government was the best form of government in the world for an intelligent people, that it ought to be kept sound and preserved forever…that the Constitution should be saved, the Union protected, and the laws revered, respected, and enforced."[xiv] Wood gave the piece to a young lawyer acquaintance, John Pitcher, who had it published. The men were amazed at the intellect and depth of this young man. Pitcher soon began loaning his law books to Lincoln.

To some of his contemporaries, Lincoln seemed to display little interest in girls during his teen years. However, those closest to him believe that his aversion was to promiscuity, and not to women, in keeping with his high moral standards. In fact, he did at times escort young ladies to social gatherings, though because he was to some extent a solitary person, he would often choose to focus on his studies rather than attend popular social events of the time.

Young Abraham was also known for his honesty, and he often acted as peacemaker wherever life took him. His stepmother Sarah commented that he "never evaded, never equivocated, never dodged."[xv] He rarely quarreled with anyone and, known for settling disputes in the family and even among his peers, his decisions were always respected. His role and reputation as a peacemaker did not hinder him from the sport of wrestling however, and for this he also earned quite a reputation. By the time he reached his full height, he was allegedly able to out-wrestle any man who cared to try it. Out of an estimated three hundred matches, he is said to have lost only one, this to Lorenzo Dow Thompson, who served with Lincoln during the Black Hawk War. The purpose of the competition was to decide which company had first choice in campsite.

The Indiana years were surely an important time for Abraham and his sister. They were old enough when they moved to remember the journey, and together they endured the loss of their mother there. As they grew, they became closer and shared even more life experiences. Abraham loved his sister deeply and was protective of her, though she was older. Sally was described as small, with eyes of dark grey, hair of brown, and very pretty. While the lives of most pioneer girls would follow a similar, more or less predetermined, pattern, the Lincolns did seek to give Sally as much education as her younger brother received. She was said to be as smart as Abraham, but did not share his intense thirst for learning, even though he encouraged her in this. To supplement the family's income, Sally hired out to another household, the Crawfords, who described her as good and kind and a hard worker.

Sally was married in Indiana, to Aaron Grigsby, the son of a prominent farmer and esteemed member of the settlement's social circle. Something came about between the Lincolns and the Grigsbys which resulted in a sort of feud between the families, though it is not known what exactly. In any case, the hard feelings were not ever resolved. When Sally was ready to give birth to her first child at the home of her father-in-law, the birth was not going well when the Grigsbys sent for a physician. The story goes that when the doctor arrived, he was so drunk that he was put immediately to bed. By then, there was not time to fetch another doctor, and Sally died giving birth to a stillborn child. Abraham was heartbroken and wept at the news. He always believed that her death was due to negligence on the part of the Grigsby family, and the incident involving the doctor was said to have fueled his interest in temperance.

In 1826, Abraham found an escape from farm work for a time to work on James Taylor's ferry operation at the mouth of the Anderson River. He was paid $6 per month plus board in return for working on the ferry and doing some clerical work for Taylor. The job actually got him in a little trouble with the law. Part of the ferrying job was to take people from the shore to board steamboats. A similar operation was conducted from the Kentucky side of the river by brothers John and Len Dill. They were said to have rights by law and that Lincoln was stealing their business, so they took him to court in Kentucky. The judge made a ruling that the law they referred to applied only when ferrying from one shore to the other, not when ferrying midway into the water to meet the steamer. Lincoln was found innocent and released. It is told that he later made friends with the judge.

Lincoln himself later told the story of earning his first dollar, to William Seward. In those days, the western rivers had no wharves, so if passengers came to the various landings, steamboats would stop and take them on board. This required, however, that the passengers find a boat and someone willing to ferry them and their trunks to the steamer so they could board. In this instance, as he was contemplating the workmanship of his first flatboat, two men with trunks arrived in carriages, spotted his flatboat, and asked who the owner was. Lincoln modestly replied that he was, and the men asked if he would give them passage to the steamer. Abraham was willing, and the men boarded. After they were aboard the steamer, Lincoln called out that the men forgot to pay him, at which time they each took a silver half dollar from their pockets and threw them onto Lincoln's flatboat. When he saw the money they had paid him, he was nearly overcome, saying that "I could scarcely believe my eyes as I picked up the money....it was a most important incident in my life...I could scarcely credit that I, the poor boy, had earned a dollar in less than a day; that by honest work I had earned a dollar. The world seemed wider and fairer before me. I was a more hopeful and thoughtful boy from that time."[xvi]

In the house where Lincoln boarded while working as a ferryman, there were many books. He is said to have read these books voraciously until midnight every evening, in order to get through all of the available books before he must leave and go on to his next job.

Another respite from farming came in 1827 when Abraham and his stepbrother, John Johnston, were hired to help build the Louisville and Portland Canal to bypass falls on the Ohio River. It was pick-and-shovel work and not easy, but the men worked for $8 to $10 per month plus board, and were paid in silver dollars.

First Flatboat Trip to New Orleans, 1828

James Gentry, who owned the largest farm in Pigeon Creek and a landing on the Ohio River, once hired Abraham, then nineteen years old, to build a flatboat and on it to take a load of produce to New Orleans. His son Allen would go along to captain the boat, while Abraham would be the crew. They set out on the 1,000 mile trip, tying up on river banks at night and floating along slowly by day. Navigating the waters was no small task. The two would have dealt with changing currents, other flatboat traffic, steamboats, and strong winds which at times would blow them all the way to the shore. They were required to give warning signals when meeting other vessels, especially at night, by waving or burning firewood or lanterns. They traveled along at about four to six miles per hour, while they fried their corn cakes, ate their pork, and washed their own shirts.

On a particular night, they tied up at the "Sugar Coast" and went to sleep, only to wake and find seven Negroes who had boarded the boat to steal the cargo and (probably) kill the crew. The story goes that Abraham, upon waking, grabbed his crab tree club and knocked some of the intruders into the river, then helped Allen chase the others into the woods. Both were injured in the incident, but apparently not seriously, and quickly cut loose and continued on their trip down the river.

In New Orleans, they sold their cargo without much trouble and thought to linger awhile to see the city. In the time that Abraham spent in this most extravagant city, he must have seen sights unfathomable to his pioneer eyes! This was a city of 40,000 people and a very active world port, exporting sugar, cotton, and tobacco to points all around the world, and importing load after load of Negro slaves. Plantation owners would come from all over to purchase slaves at auction for their huge cotton plantations, then lead them off in chains. Besides the commerce that was such a big part of the activity, the young pioneers would have set their eyes on thousands of sights they could not even have dreamed of: saloons, prostitutes, rampant gambling, blocks of shacks and hovels, and these alongside cathedrals and mansions, with none of the rawness of the pioneer settlements they had grown up in. The languages they heard were French, Spanish, and Creole, which must have seemed puzzling to the young men who spoke only "frontier" English.

Mr. Gentry had provided for the two to return home by steamboat via the Mississippi River, and they soon boarded for home. In all, the trip took about three months, and Abraham earned $8 per month for a total of $24, which he was required by law to pay over to his father, since he was not yet of age. It is impossible to measure the effect that the trip itself and the sights and sounds he experienced had on him and the direction of his life. One thing is sure; he had plenty to ponder on the long trip back home to Indiana.

Chapter 5: Move to Illinois

In 1830, once again Thomas Lincoln set out to move his family. Both dreading and fearing another round of the milk sickness and bilious fever that had killed so many of his family and neighbors, the family packed their belongings and moved out for their journey to Central Illinois. Tom's farm had not been doing well, and he had received good reports from John Hanks, a cousin of Nancy Lincoln's who had previously settled there, of better land and crops. There were thirteen in all who made the trip, including Tom and Sarah, Abraham, Dennis Hanks, Levi Hall, and certain of Tom's stepchildren with their families.

As Abraham prepared to leave with his family, he said goodbye to more than Indiana. He was leaving his childhood behind. He would leave behind two graves, one his dear mother's, and one where his beloved sister was more recently laid to rest. Later in life, when John Scripps would attempt to help write Lincoln's biography, Abraham was hesitant to discuss his childhood. "Why Scripps," he said, "it is a great piece of folly to attempt to make anything out of my early life. It can all be condensed into a single sentence, and that sentence you will find in Gray's Elegy: 'The short and simple annals of the poor.' That's my life, and that's all you or anyone else can make of it."[xvii]

The Indiana farm was sold to Charles Grigsby for $125 cash. Beginning in the winter of 1829, the men built three wagons all made of wood, including the pegs and cleats, and began packing their goods. They were ready to set out on March 1, 1830, at which time Abraham had reached the age of majority. At age 21, he could now vote and was no longer bound by law to pay his wages over to his father.

The journey commenced with two wagons pulled by two yoke of oxen and the other by four horses. At night they stopped, ate, and slept, then began again at sunrise. The ground still froze at night, causing the animals to slip and slide, thereby wreaking havoc on the wagon axles and wooden pegs. The journey was described as slow and tiresome. When crossing some rivers and creeks, they at times broke through the ice. Lincoln told the story of his little dog jumping off the wagon and falling through the ice at one point, and he waded waist deep into the icy water to save him. After the dog was rescued and returned to the wagon, he refused to leave it even after dry ground was reached. Lincoln pulled him out and set him down where he reportedly "cut joyous capers" then lay down at his master's feet for a moment before taking off again. "I guess that I felt about as glad as the dog," Lincoln added.[xviii]

Many challenges other than the cold, rain, and ice accompanied the group as they journeyed. At one point, Lincoln's trousers were so torn they became nearly useless. Sarah finally rummaged through their goods and found an old pair of Tom's for him to wear. If not for the terrible weather, the sight of Abraham wearing his father's trousers might have been amusing. At six feet, four inches, he was nearly a foot taller than Tom so most of his lower legs were exposed. Still, he walked through icy brush while driving the oxen, and his shoes were not much better than his pants.

At least one section of the journey followed what was called a "corduroy" road (made of logs laid over a pathway through a swamp), a rugged and particularly horrid experience when traveling in wagons with iron or wooden wheels and nothing to work as a shock absorber. Additionally, the road was often underwater due to flooding and the only way to keep to the unseen path was to look for posts or stakes along the roadside. Even the oxen, which were usually rugged work animals, began to balk at the conditions, and had to be whipped or otherwise coaxed to continue through the water and ice.

Dennis Hanks recalled the journey, "Abe cracked a joke every time he cracked a whip, an' he found a way out o' every tight place while the rest of us was standin' 'round scratchin' our fool heads. I reckon Abe an' Aunt Sairy run that movin', an' good thing they did, or it'd 'a' been run into a swamp an' sucked under."[xix] It was said that in those days the sight of such a caravan on the prairies was a common one, as new settlers flooded the territory.

Prior to leaving Indiana, Abraham had worked as a store clerk and, fancying himself a businessman now, thought to buy up $30 worth of goods that he might sell along the way to the new territory. While the store owner was happy to sell him the goods, he thought little of Abraham's plan or ability to sell these things across the wilderness. The 225 mile trip lasted two weeks, and at the end Abraham penned a letter to the storeowner with a report that he had not only sold all of the goods but had doubled his money!

The first sight of the Grand Prairie was an eyeful—a vast, flat landscape without slope or hill, straight to the horizon; grass that was six to eight feet high with roots so tough, even trees could not grow. The settlers remarked that the sod was tough enough to break a plow, but once the land was prepared, the returns were amazing. Seed corn was said to yield 50 bushels per acre, wheat 25-30 bushels, and oats 40-60 bushels.

In Macon County, the group met up with John Hanks, who had chosen a site for their settlement, a land with both prairie and timber. Hanks had gone to the trouble of cutting logs for their cabin, so they were able to finish it quickly, with a barn and smokehouse to boot. The ambitious workers also cleared fifteen acres and fenced it. Fences were extremely important in this area and time; land that wasn't fenced, even if it had been purchased, was considered "common" and folks could help themselves to the animals or crops which were unprotected and uncontained.

A vicious winter ensued, with blizzards, snow, rain, and ice. Unable to protect the livestock, wolves ravaged the cattle and the deer population as well. The fodder crops were ruined. Horses died in the field. With travel impossible, connections with neighbors, mills, and others were lost. The settlers endured countless days of below zero temperatures. Many families survived on parched corn. Some died from the cold or hunger, unable to get firewood or food. The survivors of the harsh winter later described themselves as "Snow Birds."

The Lincoln family was among this group, but they had it hard, lacking in meat, corn, and wood. Illness struck once again—this time fever and ague—and a store record showed the family purchasing large quantities of a remedy made of whiskey combined with Peruvian bark. Reportedly, after the sickness, "you felt as though you had gone through some sort of a collision, threshing machine, or jarring machine, and came out not killed, but next thing to it."[xx]

When the spring thaw finally came, the prairies were covered in water for miles around. Tom was convinced after a year of the snow and ague that he had made a mistake in moving there. At the first opportunity, the family and others who had journeyed with them from Indiana started the trip back. This time, the family would be absent from their son Abraham, who had set out on his own. Journeying southeast for a time, they stopped in Coles County and, after meeting up with others from Tom's family, determined to settle there instead of continuing on to Indiana. It was here that Tom and Sarah Lincoln would spend the rest of their lives.

Chapter 6: Lincoln Comes of Age

In the summer of 1830, having reached the age of 21, Abraham Lincoln set out on his own, empty-handed, with "no trade, no profession, no spot of land, no patron, no influence."[xxi] It would seem a dismal plight for anyone other than this young man. However, he soon gained a reputation for his size, strength, and work ethic. But though his strength and size made him popular, it was his good nature, quick wit, debating, and storytelling skills that drew people to him. Regardless, it was through hard manual labor that he began to make his living—rail-splitting, plowing, lumbering, boating, storekeeping—but he was thankful if he earned enough for room and board. Still in need of a new pair of pants, he bartered with a member of the Hanks family—one yard of brown jean cloth in exchange for splitting four hundred rails.

After the hard work of settling into the Illinois territory, Abraham began taking to the stump and making his first political speech, this time to humans and not to trees, rows of crops, or captive workers. When he heard two legislative candidates speak at a campaign meeting in Decatur, he stood up to propose his own ideas for improving navigation of the Sangamon River.

The tall stranger was described at this time by pioneers in the new territory as "a tall, gaunt young man, dressed in a suit of blue homespun jeans…and breeches which came to within four inches of his feet."[xxii] In fact it seemed a common belief among family acquaintances that the biggest challenge his parents had in raising him was keeping him in pants that fit his long legs. He was also said to be big-boned and strong, with a "homely face and dark skin. His hair was black and coarse, and stood on end."[xxiii]

In August of 1830, in preparation for the state elections, the Decatur precinct voters wanted to change their polling place. Abraham and many of his relatives signed a petition to the Macon County Court to make the request. Ironically, neither Abraham nor any of his party had qualified as voters yet because they had not resided in the state for six months. Nevertheless, the petition was received, considered, and the request was granted. Macon County at this time was strong Democratic territory.

Also around this time, an event is reported to have occurred in which Lincoln was plowing nearby when he heard a commotion from the town square in Decatur. Itching to investigate, he stopped the animals and walked into town where he discovered that two candidates for Illinois state representative had come to do some campaigning. John Posey, a Democrat, was speaking from his wagon and railing against the Whigs. William Lee Davidson Ewing, the incumbent and clerk of the Illinois house of representatives at the time, was from Fayette County and very popular with the people. He also made a speech that day. Abraham's cousin John Hanks thought Posey's speech bad and said Abraham could do better, so he turned down a box and Lincoln made a rebuttal to both Posey and Ewing. The crowd was delighted, and Hanks said that both candidates complimented Lincoln.

The first document known to indicate community respect for Abraham Lincoln was dated December 1830. Lincoln had provided an appraised value of a stray horse, so that the justice of the peace could properly advertise and find the owner. Though it seems a very minor thing, it was a mark of respect to be chosen to do it at all.

In the winter of 1830, Abraham did rail splitting for Sheriff William Warnick. While doing this work, he had a couple of close calls—one in which he nearly cut off his thumb while sharpening a wedge on a log, and one in which he suffered severe frostbite. Subzero temperatures that winter had frozen the Sangamon River. While attempting to walk across the iced river, Abraham fell through. The water was shallow, but his feet had become soaked in the freezing weather, and he had to walk two miles through snow back to Warnick's place. The sheriff's wife quickly doctored the frostbite with local remedies, but the damage was so severe that Lincoln spent four weeks in bed. During this recovery, he began reading Warnick's copy of the Illinois statutes.

Second Flatboat Trip to New Orleans, 1831

In the winter of 1830-31, Abraham, along with his stepbrother John Johnston and John Hanks, hired out to Denton Offutt to take a flatboat from Beardstown, Illinois down to New Orleans. When Offutt was unable to acquire a boat at Beardstown, he paid the trio to build the boat that they would take down the river. The men were paid $12 per month to acquire timber from government land and build a flatboat that was 80 by 18 feet in size. The logs to build the boat were, in fact, stolen from "Congress land" — land that was owned by the U. S. Government but not for sale to settlers or spectators yet. It was illegal to steal the timber, but also quite common to do so. By some accounts, it took about two weeks to steal an adequate number of trees for the job. The trees were then taken to the mill at Sangamon Town to be cut into planks. While waiting for this to be done, the crew lived in a small shanty they built and Abraham served as cook. An observer, Caleb Carman, watched the activities of the men and began playing cards with them to pass the time, a game called Seven-up, of which Carman remarked, "Abe played a good game."[xxiv]

The people of the village would also come out and watch the building operation. Some pitched in and helped, of whom John Roll was one. Roll remarked laughingly that his help should assure him a patronage job if Lincoln ever became president. Abraham promised it, also laughingly. While building the boat, Lincoln was part of yet another petition, this time to ask the Sangamon County Court to fill a vacant constable position. In this case, Lincoln even signed for his crewmates, John Hanks and John Johnston, proving that not only could a non-resident submit and sign a petition, but also that standards for verifying such information in those days were quite loose.

In about four weeks the boat was finally completed on the banks of the Sangamon River, which also turned out to be ample time for Abraham to endear himself to the villagers with his stories! There was storage both above and below deck, with space for the crew to sleep below. When it was time to load the cargo, Abraham drew in the farmers to help with never-ending stories and jokes. The cargo consisted of live hogs, corn, and pork barrels. The approximately fifteen hundred bushels of corn at ten cents per bushel were expected to sell for fifty cents each in New Orleans.

Prior to setting off on the trip, a bit of drama occurred which Lincoln found himself in the center of. Some of his boat-building friends were helping him to fashion a dugout or canoe to take along with the flatboat. It was a cold April day and the river was high and lively. They soon found a log and went to work with axes to hollow it out. When it was time to try it out, they threw the makeshift boat into the river and two of them jumped in right after. However, they were unable to overcome the strong current and soon found themselves in the river with the boat floating off downstream. At Abraham's quick direction, they were able to swim to an elm tree that was growing up out of the river. While they clung for life, freezing and chilled, he found a log and a rope, straddled the log in the water and made his way to the tree where the two were able to grab the rope and with Abraham's help make it back to the bank. By then, many of the villagers had gathered to witness the daring rescue and cheered the tall stranger for his act of bravery.

The crew was finally ready to embark on the journey to New Orleans in mid-April of 1831. They boarded and pushed off, and had only traveled a very small distance when again they met with some unwelcome adventure. The boat became stuck on a mill-dam at New Salem, and hung there for about twenty-four hours, bow in the air, stern in the water, and cargo slowly shifting backward. The boat must have resembled a teeter-totter, with the dam as the fulcrum. When the bow tilted down, the water below deck would run to the bow end. Soon the citizens of New Salem were gathering to view the curiosity and, as crowds will sometimes do, began to shout advice and instructions to the crew for relieving the boat of its predicament. It soon became apparent, however, that the tall dark crew member on board was paying them no mind, as he methodically began to remove the cargo onto the bank, and drill a hole in the extended end to drain the water and right the boat. Then, it was only a matter of plugging the hole, reloading the cargo, and going on their way. The spectators were awed at the ingenuity and quick thinking of this young man, but none happier than the boat's owner, who immediately vowed to build a steamboat and make Abraham Lincoln its captain! Ironically, the legality of the dam was in question at the time, and one of the first cases Abraham Lincoln would defend as an attorney involved a flatboat that sank after snagging on a river dam.

The boat and crew would have taken a route something like this: down the Sangamon River to the Illinois River, on to the Mississippi River and New Orleans, with stops at Memphis, Vicksburg, and Natchez between. The crew reportedly heard both alligators and panthers at night, surely a frightening experience before the days of electrical lighting.

The crew was able to make the rest of the journey without incident, arriving in New Orleans in May of 1831. The young men must have had a thrill a minute to see the activity and throngs of people there. It was a booming time for the town, with bustling commerce drawing crowds of merchants from practically all over the world at that time. No other area was growing at such a rate. The population was diverse: Creoles and Americans prevailed, with Germans, French, Spanish, Negroes, and Indians also thrown into the mix. How the sounds of the different languages must have tickled Lincoln's ears! The newness alone must have been more than he could even comprehend. The boat was tied up with literally thousands of others — it was said that one could walk a mile or more stepping on the tops of boats before ever touching the shore. There is no doubt that Abraham would have been sharply impressed by all he saw.

Among the sights and sounds, he was sure to have seen Negro slaves walking the streets, some in chains on their way to the dreadful slave market. Abraham may have seen them whipped, poked, and prodded like animals, or worse. He must have seen the emotions in the eyes of those who were brave enough to lift them—terror, helplessness, anger, the fear of the unknown. In their fallen countenances he must have read untold stories of betrayal and torture and degradation, of being snatched away from their families and culture to be treated cruelly. Was it these faces and tortured spirits that he saw in his mind's eye when he later led the country in a civil war? When he signed the Emancipation Proclamation?

It was apparently more than he could easily bear, both emotionally and intellectually. He likely saw advertisements such as these:

"I will at all times pay the highest cash prices for Negroes of every description, and will also attend to the sale of Negroes on commission, having a jail and yard fitted up expressly for boarding them."

"Wanted—I want to purchase twenty-five likely Negroes, between the ages of 18 and 25 years, male and female, for which I will pay the highest prices in cash." [xxv]

He was so revolted by the scene of a mulatto girl being auctioned that he left with a "deep feeling of unconquerable hate," telling his companions, "Boys, let's get away from this. If I ever get a chance to hit that thing [meaning slavery], I'll hit it hard!"[xxvi] If they only knew then what he was destined to do! John Hanks said of the slave market that Abe's heart bled for them, and though he didn't say much he was thoughtful and sad. However, as he became more and more angry about it, he began to be more outspoken, so much so that Hanks began to be concerned for their safety, saying, "His talk agin slavery right down thar amongst it…we were afeared of gettin' into trouble about his talkin' so much, and we coaxed him with all our might to be quieter-like down thar, for it wouldn't do any good nohow."[xxvii]

While the sights and sounds of New Orleans were certainly a novelty to him, he was not willing to stay there for long. After about a month, the group was ready to leave it all behind for home.

Chapter 7: New Salem Days

Upon returning from New Orleans, Offutt hired Abraham to clerk at his store and mill in New Salem, so it was here that he settled for a time. He was paid $15 per month and lived in the back room. As a store clerk, Abraham was a natural. Stores in those days weren't just businesses that sold goods; they were much, much more. These were gathering places, intellectual and social centers of the day, where folks would meet and talk about current events, politics, religion, sports, and tell jokes and stories. For this, the tall young man was more than well suited. He was also honest to a fault, having reportedly walked three miles after closing the store one night to return 6¼ cents to a patron that he had inadvertently overcharged. Nonetheless, within a few months the business failed and Abraham moved on.

The story is told of a man named Charlie Revis who would often come into Offutt's store while Abraham was the clerk there. Revis had been employed on a keel-boat for a time and as such had acquired the habit of using profanity. He would come to the store to sit and tell his stories, as was the custom in those days. Lincoln had warned the man many times about swearing in the store when ladies were present. On a particular day, a couple of ladies were shopping and Revis was chattering on and continued to spew his oaths nearly every other word. Coming to the end of his patience, Abraham took Revis outside, threw him to the ground, and placed his foot on the man's chest while he gathered smartweed. He then rubbed Revis's face, eyes, and mouth with the smelly weed until he yelled and promised Lincoln he would never swear again. After that day, those closest to Revis said they never heard him swear again!

In the village of New Salem, on August 1, 1831 Abraham cast his first ballot and happened upon another job on Election Day when the clerk's assistant was ill. At the time, he was boarding in the home of John Camron and his eleven daughters. The polling place on this occasion was actually in Camron's home. Voters in this day and time would cast their votes orally and it would be recorded by a clerk on "poll sheets" in their presence. He voted for a Henry Clay Whig for Congress and against Joseph Duncan, the incumbent. Lincoln thoroughly enjoyed lingering around the poll, aiding the clerk, meeting the New Salem residents, and taking in the whole process.

During the time he lived in John Camron's home, he heard the history of the village of New Salem, how it was a young village built on hope and promise. It had only been a couple years prior that Camron and his partner James Rutledge received permission from the state legislature to build the mill-dam that had once snagged Lincoln's flatboat. In December of that year, they sold the first lot for $12.50 and on Christmas day opened the first post office. Very soon there were twenty-five families who lived in and around the new settlement. Farther north in Illinois there was another new village springing up at about the same time. This one would be called Chicago, and the huge stretch of prairie between the two villages was yet to be tamed.

Also while at New Salem, he took it upon himself to learn some grammar. He was able to acquire a copy of Kirkham's Grammar and with a little help from his teacher friend Mentor Graham was able to complete the exercises and accomplish his goal. It was thought by some that his eagerness to learn grammar indicated he was already considering a legal or political career. He soon began to realize that people seemed to listen to him, and his speaking ability was as good as, or better than, some of those stump speeches he heard from local or traveling politicians. His friends and acquaintances encouraged him to seek public office and, perhaps from their prompting or simply because of his own interest, he began participating in debating clubs in order to improve himself. It is said that he opened his first speech with something of an apology, being unsure of himself; however, the president of the debating society, James Rutledge, remarked that there was "more than wit and fun in Abe's head."[xxviii]

Robert Rutledge said of Abraham when he first came to New Salem, that he "was all life and animation, seemed to see the bright side of every picture." The people of New Salem took the young man under their collective wings, and helped him any way they could. The women would sew and mend for him and provide meals. A village philosopher of sorts, Jack Kelso, introduced him to the writings of the English dramatist William Shakespeare and the Scottish poet Robert Burns. These would be counted among Lincoln's favorite authors.

The New Salem villagers were regularly calling on him to sign as witness on their legal documents. Though this may have been due to his known writing ability, and his availability and willingness to sign, still he must have been well thought of for the people to seek him out. In the winter of 1831-32, Abraham got his hands on a book of legal forms, studied it, and began writing his own legal documents by hand, offering his services to the people of New Salem. There was no attorney in the town, with the nearest one located in Springfield. Folks also began seeking his services in lawsuits they were involved in. His friend, Bowling Green, a justice of the peace, was helping him to lay the groundwork for a legal career. He allowed Lincoln to argue cases in his court at times—at first more for amusement, but he soon gained respect for his skill. Lincoln did not accept pay for his services, perhaps due to charity, perhaps from fear of retribution for practicing law without a license!

Abraham was also known to have judged some sporting events, such as horse racing. It is said that his fairness in these ventures gave him the nickname Honest Abe. A horse race official said of him, "Lincoln is the fairest man I ever had to deal with. If Lincoln is in this country when I die I want him to be my administrator, for he is the only man I ever met with that was wholly and purely and unselfishly honest."[xxix]

As Lincoln participated more in public speaking and debating, and attending discussions in and around the New Salem area, the subject of slavery would arise frequently. For good or for bad, Lincoln's views were becoming public.

On March 9, 1832, Lincoln wrote perhaps the most important thing he had written to date when he announced to the public that he would be a candidate for the Illinois State Legislature. The writing was printed in Springfield's *Sangamo Journal* and also issued as a handbill. While he came across as somewhat awkward about stepping into this arena, he nevertheless was sure of his platform and was a most willing debater.

He ran on a platform strongly against a railroad for New Salem, and strongly in favor of improved navigation of the Sangamon River and steamboat traffic. He was also a strong proponent of religion, scriptures, morality, books and education. He proposed usury laws, which seemed at the time to be aimed at certain people, though he named no one. Lincoln directed his ideas toward the independent voters, commenting that "if the good people in their wisdom shall see fit to keep me in the background, I have been too familiar with disappointments to be very much chagrined."[xxx]

Ironically, at about this same time, around March of 1832, the first steamboat made its way up the Sangamon River, after Lincoln and a crew came to the rescue of the boat by clearing snags and overhanging branches to make way. At New Salem and other points along the way, curious and exciting onlookers cheered the boat on as far as Portland Landing, seven miles north of Springfield. The steamer was *Talisman* and it came bearing goods "direct from the East." The occasion was celebrated by a reception and dance at the county courthouse.

Chapter 8: Black Hawk War

An official messenger from Governor John Reynolds arrived in New Salem in April of 1832, calling for four hundred volunteers from the Sangamon County state militia to report to Beardstown on April 24. Once again, it appeared there would be a war with the Indians, namely Black Hawk who was the 67 year old war leader of the Sac and Fox tribes. Back in 1804 the tribes had been relocated west of the Mississippi River and Black Hawk, having had plenty of time to mull this over, determined to return and reclaim the northern Illinois territory, claiming that his people had been treated wrongly and further asserting that "land can not be sold,"[xxxi] but only those things that can be carried away. Having experienced earlier encounters with the war leader, the settlers were panicked at his return, and rightly so. A prior appearance by the old warrior left a trail of cruel destruction; hence, the call to arms.

Upon hearing the call for volunteers, Lincoln responded. Offutt's store was failing and the man had seemingly left New Salem for other pursuits and, thinking that he would be jobless and homeless, rode to Richland Creek on a borrowed horse where he met up with a company of friends and neighbors to volunteer. In these days, Illinois state law required all males aged 18 to 45 to drill twice a year or else pay a fine of one dollar; as one dollar was not easy to come by in that time, everyone drilled. Though Lincoln was not quite knowledgeable of military ways, his company nonetheless "elected" him as captain. Lincoln considered this a great honor, later saying that he had not "had any success in life which gave him so much satisfaction."[xxxii]

He may have had some regrets early on about being the captain of this ragtag group of men. It is reported that in response to his first order, one man responded, "Go to hell." The group was disorderly, poorly disciplined, and grumbled about living conditions before even seeing any combat. However, they marched on to Beardstown to join an army of about 1,600 troops there. On May 9, 1832 they were officially sworn into federal service. Being unfamiliar with the military lifestyle, Lincoln got himself into some trouble. In one incident, his sword was taken away when he fired his gun inside camp, probably for fun. Another time, his company of misfits helped themselves to the officers' whiskey supply and they were so drunk the next morning they missed the order to fall in and march. For this indiscretion, Lincoln was required to wear a wooden sword for two days.

In time, his company came to admire and obey him. On May 12 they reached Dixon on the Rock River, but it was a treacherous journey. Provisions were inadequate. The men waded through mud for miles and miles, swam rivers, and were hardly ever dry. It was a high price to pay for a war which turned out to be somewhat of a debacle.

Black Hawk himself, prior to this mission to reclaim the land, had been promised provisions and warriors from the other tribes and also from the British, whom he had befriended and aided in the War of 1812. When none came, the leader had decided to give up the quest and return back west. Before he could begin the trip back, he heard the soldiers were nearby and sent an envoy of three braves with a white flag to request a meeting and permission to descend the river. They were followed by a second group of five braves to observe the proceedings and report back. The story goes that when the first group arrived at camp, the soldiers, by then partly drunk, reacted by rushing them and running them into the camp. Seeing the second group, they gave chase and killed two of them. The three who escaped returned to Black Hawk and made their report. The tribal leader was furious and quickly rallied his group of forty braves to take revenge. He did not stop to think that he was vastly outnumbered, but began attacking. The company of soldiers then panicked and fled, passing their camp and returning the full twelve miles back to Dixon, where they reported being attacked by 2,000 savages.

Black Hawk continued on his warpath, leaving a trail of burned cabins, slaughtered livestock, and the scalps of white men. The governor had dispatched even more troops in search of Black Hawk, but he was elusive. Meanwhile, the volunteers became so dissatisfied that Governor Reynolds released them from service. In late May however, some troops were still needed and a few volunteered to stay on, of whom Lincoln was one, this time as a private. He was then part of the Independent Rangers under the command of Captain Elijah Iles, who would be used as messengers and scouts; however the group was mustered out again in June. On June 20, Lincoln mustered in once again, this time under the command of Captain Jacob Early, and this was where Lincoln saw the most action, though he was not involved in any direct fighting with the Indians. His group moved up the Rock River after mid-June, and it was here they came upon the site of the skirmish at Kellogg's Grove, one of the bloodiest of the war. Lincoln and his unit helped to bury the five soldiers who had been killed by Black Hawk's warriors. Lincoln would later say of the incident, "I remember just how those men looked as we rode up the little hill....The red light of the morning sun was streaming upon them as they lay, heads toward us, on the ground. And every man had a round red spot on the top of his head, about as big as a dollar, where the redskins had taken his scalp."[xxxiii] Once again, Black Hawk and his men had eluded the soldiers.

The Kellogg's Grove skirmish did claim the life of at least one young Indian chief, and upon discovering his remains, Lincoln encouraged pursuit. One fellow militiaman remembered, "When fighting was expected or danger apprehended Lincoln was first to say, 'Let's go.'"[xxxiv] However, it seemed the militia was being badly and shamefully beaten by this band of Indians and, in fact, the settlers began to be perplexed, and no doubt a little apprehensive, at the seeming ineffectiveness of the soldiers. Time marched on, and July consisted of marching through forests and swamps in what would later become the state of Wisconsin. Lincoln's company was once again disbanded and this time headed for home. Ironically, a few days later the final battle would be fought where most of the Indians were killed.

Chapter 9: Return to New Salem

Abraham Lincoln returned home to New Salem after his brief military stint, with only a few days left until the election. He switched gears immediately and began his electioneering. Almost everyone in New Salem supported Lincoln, regardless of party affiliation. Elections then were purely personal and because Lincoln was well liked, he enjoyed their support in the campaign though he never missed an opportunity to hop up on the stump. As it turned out, he was defeated in this election; however this would be "the only time he was ever defeated on a direct vote of the people."[xxxv]

With his first election behind him, Lincoln began the search for his next job. He applied to several New Salem stores for a clerk position but was not hired. Deciding to purchase a store for himself—quite an interesting and ambitious undertaking considering he was practically penniless—he first bought out a partner who owned a store with William Berry. This set into motion a series of events which culminated in Lincoln and Berry owning three stores and a monopoly on the New Salem grocery business. The partnership would not last, however. Lincoln's new partner proved to be a heavy drinker, gambler, and fighter—quite the opposite of Lincoln's mild mannered personality. Abraham initially trusted Berry a little too much and soon realized that the profits were being squandered whilst he lay in the shade of a tree or on a store counter reading Shakespeare or Burns.

Though Lincoln apparently did not have the best business sense, while tending the stores he began to improve himself in order to pursue a legal career. He began to study the law in earnest, beginning with the statutes of Indiana, which also included a copy of the U.S. Declaration of Independence and the Constitution. He tells the story of a fellow with a loaded wagon passing through town who had a barrel that wouldn't fit and, needing to rid himself of it, asked Lincoln to buy it from him. Lincoln, wishing to show charity to the man, paid him a half dollar and placed the barrel in a back room of the store. Sometime later, he was cleaning up and came upon the forgotten barrel. Lincoln emptied the barrel only to find, stuffed in the bottom, a complete edition of Blackstone's *Commentaries on the Laws of England*. He began to read and would later say, "Never in my whole life was my mind so thoroughly absorbed. I read until I devoured them."[xxxvi] Abraham Lincoln—pioneer, farmer, rail splitter, clerk, boatman, soldier, aspiring politician, entrepreneur, and student extraordinaire—had found his next career.

Perhaps it was the native pioneer spirit within Abraham Lincoln which made him seem a drifter of sorts—moving from one job to the next, appearing lazy or disinterested in what seemed normal work to most people, and always willing to tell a joke, spin a yarn, or make a speech at the drop of a hat. Perhaps he was driven by the inner voice which convinced him that he was destined for greatness, or at least something more than a pioneer farmer. Regardless, he did become great despite some pretty unfavorable odds. Something came from deep down inside the young boy that drove him to achieve an education when none was readily available. He did not allow his humble beginnings to define the man he became, though they surely helped to mold him. He saw the value in books and learning, and he found a way to use his intellect to improve himself, make a living, and leave the world a little better for having lived in it.

Notes

---

[i] Carl Sandburg. *Abraham Lincoln: The Prairie Years*. New York: Harcourt, Brace & World, Inc., 1954. p. 3.

[ii] William Lawrence Miller. *Lincoln and His World*. Mechanicsburg, PA: Stackpole Books, 2003. p. 16.

[iii] Miller, p. 17.

[iv] Ida M. Tarbell and J. McCan Davis. *The Early Life of Abraham Lincoln*. New York: S.S. McClure, 1896. Kindle file.

[v] Tarbell and Davis, Kindle file.

[vi] Sandburg, p. 13.

[vii] Sandburg, p. 13.

[viii] Sandburg, p. 13.

[ix] Ward Hill Lamon, and Rodney O. Davis.

The Life of Abraham Lincoln. Lincoln: University of Nebraska Press, 1999. Digital file.

[x] Lamon and Davis, Digital file.

[xi] Lamon and Davis, Digital file.

[xii] Sandburg, p. 10.

[xiii] Tarbell and Davis, Kindle file.

[xiv] Miller, p. 68.

[xv] Miller, p. 71.

[xvi] Tarbell and Davis, Kindle file.

[xvii] Miller, p. 89.

[xviii] Miller, p. 93.

[xix] Miller, p. 93.

[xx] Miller, p. 94.

[xxi] Tarbell and Davis, Kindle file.

[xxii] Tarbell and Davis, Kindle file.

[xxiii] "Lincoln, Abraham." *World Book Online InfoFinder.* World Book, 2014. Web. 16 Apr. 2014.

[xxiv] Miller, p. 101.

[xxv] Sandburg, p. 23.

[xxvi] Tarbell and Davis, Kindle file.

[xxvii] Miller, p. 109.

[xxviii] Sandburg, p. 26.

[xxix] Miller, p. 120.

[xxx] Sandburg, p. 28.

[xxxi] Sandburg, p. 29.

[xxxii] Miller, p. 158.

[xxxiii] Miller, p. 176.

[xxxiv] Miller, p. 176.

[xxxv] Tarbell and Davis, Kindle file.

[xxxvi] Tarbell and Davis, Kindle file.

Works cited

Lamon, Ward Hill, and Rodney O Davis. *The Life Of Abraham Lincoln*. Lincoln: University of Nebraska Press, 1999. Digital file.

"Lincoln, Abraham." *World Book Online InfoFinder.* World Book, 2014. Web. 16 April 2014.

Miller, Richard Lawrence. *Lincoln And His World*. Mechanicsburg, PA: Stackpole Books, 2006. Print.

Remsburg, John B. *Abraham Lincoln: Was He a Christian?* New York: The Truth Seeker Company, 1893. Digital file.

Sandburg, Carl. *Abraham Lincoln*. 1st ed. New York: Harcourt, Brace, 1954. Print.

Tarbell, Ida M, and J. McCan Davis. *The Early Life Of Abraham Lincoln*. 1st ed. New York, N.Y.: S.S. McClure, 1896. Kindle file.

Made in the USA
San Bernardino, CA
09 July 2020